Wild About Wheels

DELIVERY TRUCKS

by Nancy Dickmann

PEBBLE
a capstone imprint

Pebble Emerge is published by Pebble, an imprint of Capstone.
1710 Roe Crest Drive
North Mankato, Minnesota 56003
www.capstonepub.com

Copyright © 2022 by Capstone. All rights reserved. No part of this publication may be reproduced in whole or in part, or stored in a retrieval system, or transmitted in any form or by any means, electronic, mechanical, photocopying, recording, or otherwise, without written permission of the publisher.

Library of Congress Cataloging-in-Publication Data
Names: Dickmann, Nancy, author.
Title: Delivery trucks / by Nancy Dickmann.
Description: North Mankato, Minnesota : Pebble, [2022] | Series: Wild about wheels | Includes bibliographical references and index. | Audience: Ages 6-8. | Audience: Grades 2-3. | Summary: "Delivery trucks carry millions of packages around the country each day. In New York City alone, 1.5 million packages are delivered every day! Young readers will learn about the types of delivery trucks, their main parts, and what they carry inside"-- Provided by publisher.
Identifiers: LCCN 2020025532 (print) | LCCN 2020025533 (ebook) | ISBN 9781977132338 (hardcover) | ISBN 9781977133274 (paperback) | ISBN 9781977154101 (ebook pdf)
Subjects: LCSH: Trucks--Juvenile literature. | Delivery of goods--Juvenile literature.
Classification: LCC TL230.15 .D53 2022 (print) | LCC TL230.15 (ebook) | DDC 629.225--dc23
LC record available at https://lccn.loc.gov/2020025532
LC ebook record available at https://lccn.loc.gov/2020025533

Image Credits
Alamy: Chuck Franklin, 18–19, Imagic Industrial, 12, Julian Kemp, 7, Justin Kase z12z, 11; Capstone Studio: Karon Dubke, 21 (art supplies); iStockphoto: THEPALMER, cover, back cover, vitranc, 6; Newscom: Reuters/Jim Young, 4; Shutterstock: Berns Images, 14, BigBlueStudio, 5, Catrin Haze, 13, elbud, 16, George Sheldon, 15, Mark LaMoyne, 17, puhhha, 8, Red Orange, 21 (drawing), Siwakorn1933, 9, Steve Skjold, 10, Tish11 (background), throughout

Editorial Credits
Editor: Amy McDonald Maranville; Designer: Cynthia Della-Rovere; Media Researcher: Eric Gohl; Production Specialist: Katy LaVigne

All internet sites appearing in back matter were available and accurate when this book was sent to press.

Table of Contents

What Delivery Trucks Do........4

Look Inside....................8

Look Outside..................14

Delivery Truck Diagram......18

Design a Delivery Truck......20

Glossary....................22

Read More 23

Internet Sites 23

Index 24

Words in **bold** are in the glossary.

What Delivery Trucks Do

A package is ready to ship. How will it get to your house? In a delivery truck!

Some packages come from far away. They may travel on a plane. They may travel in a large truck. The package gets to a **delivery center**. Then a delivery truck brings it to you!

Some people cannot go to a store. They might live far away. They might not have a car. Delivery trucks help. They bring people the things they need.

People can have lots of things delivered. Delivery trucks carry books and clothes. They bring flowers and food. They can even bring large things such as washing machines.

Look Inside

The driver sits in the cab. It is at the front of the truck. The truck's controls are here. The driver uses a steering wheel and pedals to drive.

The driver has a device in the cab. It is like a smartphone. It lists all the stops. It plans a **route** and shows a map. The device keeps track of the packages. The driver **scans** each one as it is delivered.

Some trucks carry food to homes. They load up in the morning. Then they drive to all the stops.

The food must be kept cold. If not, it will go bad. The truck has a cooling system. It is like a giant fridge. Some trucks have a place to put frozen food too.

Trucks can carry hundreds of packages. The packages go on shelves in the back of the trucks. But many packages look alike. How can the driver find the right one?

The driver puts the packages in order. Those that will be delivered first go at one end. Packages that will be delivered last go at the other end.

Look Outside

Not all delivery trucks are the same. They come in different shapes and sizes. Vans often deliver small packages. Box trucks can carry big items. They have lots of space in the back.

Many delivery trucks are painted with the company's name or **logo**. They might have **ads** on the sides.

roll-up door

Some trucks have a roll-up door. The door is made of strips called **slats**. The driver pushes the door up. There is a strap to help pull it down again.

16

This kind of truck often has a **dolly** on board. The driver can load it with packages and wheel it to the front door.

dolly

Delivery Truck Diagram

cab

company logo

Design a Delivery Truck

Pretend that you are a delivery driver. Can you design a truck? Think about what you would deliver. Would you need a big truck or a van? Sketch your design.

Glossary

ad (AD)—information that tells people about a company or product

cab (KAB)—the compartment at the front of a vehicle where the driver sits

delivery center (de-LIV-ur-ee SEN-tur)—a place where items are sorted and sent out for delivery

dolly (DAH-lee)—a small cart with two wheels and handles for moving heavy things

logo (LOH-go)—a company symbol used in advertising

route (ROOT)—the path that a delivery truck follows to reach all of its stops

scan (SKAN)—to use a scanning tool to take a picture or to track or get information

slat (SLAT)—a thin piece of metal or wood that overlaps with or fits together with other pieces

Read More

Meister, Cari. *Guinness World Records: Wacky Wheels.* New York: Harper, an imprint of Harper Collins Publishers, 2016.

Murray, Julie. *Mail Trucks.* Minneapolis: Abdo Kids, 2016.

Schuh, Mari. *Trucks.* North Mankato, MN: Capstone Press, 2018.

Internet Sites

How Stuff Works: How UPS Works
money.howstuffworks.com/ups.htm

Kiddle: Truck Facts for Kids
kids.kiddle.co/Truck

Index

ads, 15

box trucks, 14

cabs, 8, 9

cooling systems, 11

dollies, 17

doors, 16, 17

food, 7, 10–11

homes, 10

logos, 15

maps, 9

packages, 5, 9, 12, 13, 14, 17

routes, 9

scanning, 9

slats, 16

straps, 16

vans, 14